The Butcher's Daughter
Part II
Written by Tommy Watkins
AF414323

Rachel was graduating college and ready to jump into the real world.

Rachel met a boy in college named Billy. Billy and Rachel soon started to date past graduation.

After a year of dating, Billy took Rachel to a nice restaurant one night and pulled out a diamond ring to propose marriage.

Rachel immediately said yes! And the entire restaurant erupted in applause

Rachel went home to tell her parents

Her parents were excited to meet Bill

The next day, Billy arrives to meet Rachel's parents.

They sit down with Billy and learn that Billy is a vegan and doesn't eat meat.

Brutus, Rachel's father, is furious! How could his daughter marry a man who doesn't eat meat! Brutus told Billy to leave his house!

It was in question whether Brutus would allow Rachel to marry Billy. Elaine, Rachel's mother, reminded Brutus that she was a vegan before they married. It took Brutus's love for Elaine to allow them to wed.

Brutus invited Billy back to the house
Brutus gave his blessing for Rachel
and Billy to be married. Despite Billy
being vegan, his love for Rachel
conquered over everything.

Rachel and Billy got married. With a vegan menu at the reception, Billy even tried meat for the first time at the wedding.

The End

www.ingramcontent.com/pod-product-compliance
Lightning Source LLC
Chambersburg PA
CBHW042136110726
48006CB00003B/901